Understanding the Crisis in Kivu :

Report of the CODESRIA Mission to the Democratic Republic of Congo September, 1997

Text of report submitted to the General Assembly of the Council for the Development of Social Research in Africa (CODESRIA) in Dakar, Senegal, December 14–18, 1998.

Mahmood Mamdani

Monograph Series 1/2001

The **CODESRIA Monograph Series** is published to stimulate debate, comments, and further research on the subjects covered. The Series will serve as a forum for works based on the findings of original research, which however are too long for academic journals but not long enough to be published as books, and which deserve to be accessible to the research community in Africa and elsewhere. Such works may be case studies, theoretical debates or both, but they incorporate significant findings, analyzes, and critical evaluations of the current literature on the subjects in question.

Understanding the Crisis in Kivu :
Report of the CODESRIA Mission to the Democratic Republic of Congo

© Council for the Development of Social Science Research in Africa, 2001
Avenue Cheikh Anta Diop X Canal IV, Dakar, Senegal, BP 3304

Typeset and printed by CODESRIA

ISBN: 2-86978-103-2

CODESRIA would like to express its gratitude to the Swedish Development Co-operation Agency (Sida/SAREC), the International Development Research Centre (IDRC), the Mac Arthur Foundation, the Carnegie Corporation, the Norwegian Ministry of Foreign Affairs, the Danish Agency for International Development (DANIDA), the French Ministry of Cooperation, the Ford Foundation, the United Nations Development Programme (UNDP), the Rockefeller Foundation, the Prince Claus Fund and the Government of Senegal for support of its research, publication and training activities.

Contents

Introduction 1

The Citizenship Question: Civic and Ethnic 1

The Crisis of Civic Citizenship 5

    The Sovereign National Conference (CNS) and the
    Resolution on Citizenship, 1991–92 9

The Crisis of Ethnic Citizenship 12

    North Kivu: The Banyaruchuru and the Banyamasis 13

    South Kivu: The Barundi and the Banyamulenge 16

Rwanda and Kivu Province 20

The Military Solution to Dictatorship 28

The Antidote to Militarism 32

Summing up the Crisis 34

Local Research Capacity 36

Recommendations 38

    Proposed Research Agenda 40

Appendix: List of Persons Interviewed 41

Author

Mahmood Mamdani is currently Professor of Anthropology and International Affairs; Columbia University. He was the A.C. Jordan Professor of African Studies and Director of the Centre for African Studies at the University of Cape Town and founder director of the Centre for Basic Research in Kampala, Uganda. He studied at University of Pittsburgh; Fletcher School of Law and Diplomacy, Tufts University, and Harvard University. Among his numerous publications are *When Victims Become Killers: Colonialisms, Nativism and the Genocide in Rwanda* (Princeton 2001), *Beyond Rights Talk and Culture Talk* (David Philip, 2000), *Citizen and Subject: Contemporary Africa and the Legacy of Late Colonialism* (Princeton University Press, 1996) and co-edited with Ernest Wamba-dia-Wamba, *African Studies in Social Movements and Democracy* (CODESRIA 1995).

Introduction

The Congo mission of CODESRIA took place in September 1997, in the interregnum between the First Rebellion against Mobutu and the Second Rebellion against Kabila. The mission comprised two members, Jacques Depelchin and Mahmood Mamdani (chair).[1]

Conceptualized as the first of a two-phased focus on the crisis in the Great Lakes region, the Congo mission was to concentrate specifically on the region of Kivu. In that context, the Mission was asked:
   a) to meet different categories of people to establish a sense of the situation on the ground;
   b) to engage local researchers with a view to recommending a research agenda directly relating to the crisis in the region;
   c) to recommend a programme of action to be followed by CODESRIA in the region.

The Congo Mission lasted 17 days, from 3 to 19 September 1997. We visited four cities—Kinshasa, Goma, Bukavu and Kisangani—and interviewed 32 persons (see Appendix). Except for one rare instance, all other interviews were jointly done by both members of the mission.

While Jacques Depelchin and I would discuss each interview as we completed it, we never really tried to arrive at a joint account of the crisis. Subsequent events in Congo, particularly the fact that Jacques is now a prominent member of the Second Rebellion (against Kabila), has made it difficult for us to meet and explore the possibility of a common account. It is for this reason that I feel compelled to take individual responsibility for the report, and particularly for the interpretative sections that follow. The following, then, is an analysis of the crisis and a framing of a research agenda and a programme of action following from that analysis.

The Citizenship Question: Civic and Ethnic

At the root of the political crisis in Congo is the crisis of the Congolese state. An analysis of state crisis, in turn, will serve to challenge two theses

---

[1] Jacques Depelchin was then part of the secretariat of the Alliance of Democratic Forces of Congo in Kinshasa.

that have become part of conventional wisdom in the analysis of contemporary African politics.

The first thesis is widely held in Pan-Africanist circles, that the root problem of the African state stems from the artificial nature of its boundaries. Were these boundaries not, after all, arbitrarily drawn up at the Berlin Conference of 1885–86 and then imposed from outside? While this cannot be denied, it is worth keeping in mind that all boundaries are more or less artificial. This is why if we want to understand the crisis of the state, an understanding of how power is organized is likely to prove a more illuminating starting point than the nature of boundaries that frame power.

The second thesis, now common in Africanist political science in North America, is that the state is collapsing in more and more African countries. The Congo is often held up as an example of this. The main problem with this thesis is that it tries to understand the state in Africa through an analogy, rather than through its own history. Instead of taking as its starting point the state created under colonialism and actually existing in Africa, this thesis presumes that the state in Africa has been an attempt to recreate the European state in African conditions. The conclusion that the attempt to imitate the original has failed has ushered in a deep sense of pessimism about African possibilities. For Afro-pessimism, the difference between the post-Westphalian state in Europe and the post-colonial state in Africa is evidence of the failure of the modernist project in Africa. It is this difference Africanist political science understands as a failure and sums up as a theory of state collapse.

The difference needs to be understood as the outcome of a different historical process, rather than as empirical evidence of a failure. The state in Africa is a product of a radically different history, a history of colonial conquest. It is at the same time Western colonialism's most creative response to the dilemma that accompanies every rule based on conquest: how do you justify rule by others? This is the dilemma that colonial theorists called 'the native question'.

The 'native question' resulted in a perennial search for legitimacy, leading to a radical recasting of the nature of colonial rule in its final phase. This reorganization of power took place in those African colonies acquired in the aftermath of the Scramble that followed the Berlin Conference of 1885. Not surprisingly, it was Britain, the leading colonial power of the time, that took the initiative to soften the alien character of colonial rule by restructuring the colonial state. Characteristically, British ideologues gave the new state structure the benign name of 'indirect rule'. The French followed suit in the 1920s, when they shifted the basis of colonial rule in their equatorial African colonies (and in Morocco) from 'assimilation' to 'association'. Belgium effected a similar shift in its African colonies in the 1930s.

It is this reform that begins to explain what is different about the state in Africa. Indirect rule reorganized the colonial space under two distinct legal regimes, one civic and the other customary. The seat of civil power was the central state. Its will was expressed through civil law. Though it claimed to speak the universal language of rights, the regime of civil rights became an exclusive privilege of the population of metropolitan origin, described as racially distinct. Natives, in contrast, were portrayed as creatures of habit, and were brought under the thumb of a Native Authority, charged with enforcing custom through a regime of customary law. This, however, did not lead to the creation of a single customary law and a single customary regime ruling all natives. Since the colonial power claimed that each ethnic group had its own distinctive custom, it created a different set of customary laws, one for each ethnic group, and established a separate Native Authority to enforce each set of laws. The result was a Janus-faced power, with two faces. The difference between them was that while civic power was racialized, the Native Authority came to be ethnicized.

This form of the state was reformed after independence. While the details of the reform varied from one country to another, one could discern two broad currents: one radical, the other conservative. The Congolese reform followed the more conservative variant: while civic power was de-racialized, the Native Authority remained ethnicized. In fact, as the Belgian circle commander withdrew at independence, the ethnic aspect of the Native Authority got further entrenched.

The distinction between civic and ethnic power allows us to identify precisely what is lost in the course of an analysis that proceeds through analogies.

When Africanists speak of the collapse of the state, they have their empirical gaze fixed on civic power. The Native Authority is beyond their sight. Yet, it is not as much the centralized civic power in the urban areas—which comprise roughly 40 per cent of the population—that has held Congo together as much as the hundreds of Native Authorities that control the bulk of the rural population in the name of enforcing 'custom'. Unlike civic power which is the urban-based central state of Congo, it is better to think of rural Congo as giant federation of Bantustans, one version of the reformed colonial state.

We shall see that the political crisis of this reformed colonial state lies in the bifurcated citizenship reproduced through the bifurcated state. This identity-formation has been the result of a two-step process. To begin with, the colonial state made a distinction in law between those indigenous and those not: as a rule, the non-indigenous belonged to the civic sphere and the indigenous to the ethnic sphere. The second step was for civil law to make a 'racial' distinction amongst the non-indigenous, between those 'white' and those not—or those considered 'civilized' and those not—and for customary law to desegregate the indigenous population ethnically, between one 'tribe' and another. We shall see how the Banyarwanda immigrants to Congo fell between the two stools of this bifurcated world. For they were both excluded from the civic space where they were considered racially 'African', and therefore 'indigenous', and from the customary space where they were considered ethnically 'non-indigenous'. Through its bifurcated legal and political apparatus, the colonial state enforced two distinct political identities: race as an identity that united the core beneficiaries of colonialism as 'white', and ethnicity as an identity that fragmented its core victims into so many 'tribes'. This outcome racialized civic identity and ethnicized native identity. It also defined the double agenda of political reform in the post-colonial period: de-racialization and de-ethnicization.

Post-colonial reform tended to cohere around a common core agenda. Everywhere, the tendency of the post-colonial state was to de-racialize civic identity. Civic citizenship ceased to recognize any difference based on race or place of origin. That is where similarities ended, for the conservative variant of the post-colonial state continued to reproduce the native identity as ethnic. The irony was that de-racialization without de-ethnicization continued to reproduce a bifurcated citizenship. This is because not everyone who was a civic citizen, a citizen of the state of Congo, had an ethnic membership of a Native Authority. While the civic sphere ceased to make a distinction between citizens who were indigenous and those who were not, the ethnic sphere continued to make this distinction. Only those considered indigenous were entitled to a Native Authority of their own, and thus to an ethnic citizenship. It is worth exploring the distinction between civic and ethnic citizenship to understand the practical significance of being a civic, but not an ethnic, citizen.

Civic citizenship is a consequence of membership of the central state. Both the qualifications for citizenship, and the rights that are its entitlement, are specified in the constitution. These rights are mainly individual, and are located in the political and civil domain. In contrast, ethnic citizenship is a result of membership in the Native Authority. It is the source of a different category of rights, mainly social and economic. Further, these rights are not accessed individually but by virtue of group membership, the group being the ethnic community. The key socio-economic right is the right to use land as a source of livelihood. Herein lies the material basis of ethnic belonging, particularly for the ethnic poor. The immediate practical consequence of being defined a citizen of non-indigenous origin is this: non-indigenous citizens are denied 'customary' access to land since they do not have their own Native Authority.

I shall argue that the cutting edge of the crisis in Kivu is the crisis of citizenship that has plagued the Kinyarwanda-speaking population in the region. At the same time, we shall see that the intensity of this crisis is a result of a confluence of two factors: the internal crisis of citizenship, and the external impact of a traumatized post-genocide Rwanda. We shall also see that the mode of their interaction has been increasingly—and adversely—shaped by the mediation of international forces, being mainly France and the United Nations. Historically divided into three major groups—the Banyamulenge, the Banyamasisi, and the Banyaruchuru—the Kinyarwanda-speaking population in the region of Kivu has over the past few years come to be defined, as in Rwanda, as two opposed identities, Hutu and Tutsi. Today, no matter where they live, the Congolese Tutsi have come to be known by a single generic name, the Banyamulenge. To fathom the depth of the citizenship crisis that affects this population, and to grasp the link between it and the crisis in Kivu, it is necessary to explore the citizenship question in both its manifestations, the civic as well as the ethnic.

The Crisis of Civic Citizenship

The historical account in this section and the next is a synthesis arrived at on the basis of discussions with university and NGO-based researchers in Goma, Bukavu and Kisangani. The question of citizenship is viewed from the standpoint of the Kinyarwanda-speaking minority because their citizenship dilemma has come to signify the contemporary crisis of citizenship in Kivu. So far as possible, I have avoided direct quotation.

When I could not resist one, I have avoided citing its author. While the appendix lists names and institutional affiliations of the people we met and interviewed, I have kept direct authorship of quotations anonymous, because we are dealing with highly unstable region undergoing a profound political crisis.

The independence of Congo was preceded by provincial and municipal elections in 1960. The Kinyarwanda-speaking population participated in these elections, both as voters and as candidates. Several candidates were elected to formal positions, suggesting that the general population had come to accept them as Congolese. This outcome, however, was not to last long.

The independence of Congo was marked by a local rebellion in North Kivu. La Guerre du Kinyarwanda was an uprising of the Kinyarwanda-speaking population against chiefly abuse. Its impact rendered the nationality status of the Kinyarwanda-speaking minority so sensitive that the Roundtable Conference in Brussels was unable to fix the juridical status of this minority even though its representatives participated in the conference. The Fundamental Law left the citizenship status of the minority unresolved, stating that the Congolese people will themselves decide this issue. Even though Mobutu abrogated the Fundamental Law when he usurped power in 1965, the Brussels outcome came to introduce an element of insecurity in the juridical status of the Kinyarwanda-speaking minority. This, in turn, became one of the factors shaping their response to the first great post-independence rebellion in the region.

The Mulelist Rebellion of 1963-64 split the population in the region along ethnic lines. Everyone—the Babembe, the Bafulira, the Bavira and the Banyamulenge—split. As some went with the state army, and others with the rebellion, a general trend developed over time. Small groups of Banyamulenge at first sided with the insurrection, in Fizi for example. But even then they insisted on autonomy, and were strongly driven by an interest in acquiring weapons to defend their cattle. In time, and as a whole, the Babembe, the Bafulira and the Bavira went with the rebellion, whereas the Banyamulenge went with the state army.

In the three decades that stretched from the end of the Mulelist Rebellion to the Beginning of the genocide in Rwanda, a complex of processes unfolded in Kivu. In retrospect, one can discern how this produced the environment that incubated the post-1994 crisis of Kivu. The more they were blocked at the local level, the more the Kinyarwanda-speaking minority looked for alternate strategies, both economic and political. Unable to access land as a 'customary' right like the 'indigenous' Congolese, they devoted resources to purchasing as much land as possible through the marked. Frustrated from exercising power locally, they made every effort to be elected at higher provincial and national levels. This, in turn, provoked a response from amongst the 'indigenous' majority. Afraid that the Banyarwanda would use national representation to acquire power locally, 'indigenous' Congolese came to oppose citizenship rights for them. When their citizenship was questioned and their right to run for office denied, the Kinyarwanda-speaking minority—and particularly the Tutsi amongst them—developed a strategy of entry into organs of the state, particularly the security apparatus.

Three key discussions on citizenship mark the course of the spiraling crisis that fed the insecurity of the Kinyarwanda-speaking minority. Each had a vital impact on the future of this minority. The first was Mobutu's 1972 Citizenship Decree. The second was the 1981 Citizenship Law passed by an elected parliament, and the third was a resolution by the 1991-92 Sovereign National Conference upholding the provisions of the 1981 Law. To understand the nature of the movement from 1972 to 1981 to 1991, we need to grasp the changing political context over these decades.

The 1972 Citizenship Decree: The context of the 1972 Citizenship Decree was the first major post-independence crisis that sent thousands of refugees streaming into Kivu. This development took place as the aftermath of the massacre of about 200,000 Hutu in Burundi in 1972. The refugee influx fed the anxieties of the local population in South Kivu, particularly those—the Bafulira, the Bavira, the Babembe—who were beginning to see themselves as an imperiled 'indigenous' majority. This majority responded with pressure on the Kinyarwanda-speaking minority. The 1972 Citizenship Decree was an attempt by the Mobutu regime to dispel the growing sense of insecurity in the Banyarwanda minority, by extending citizenship to those who had come as refugees from Rwanda in 1959-60. But the effect was the opposite. It alarmed the local majority who saw the Decree as a direct outcome of growing Tutsi influence within the state apparatus. In this instance, it was believed that the Decree was signed by Mobutu under the influence of Bisengimana, his *Chef de Cabinet* (Chief private Secretary) who was himself said to be a 1959 Tutsi refugee. In North Kivu, where the Kinyarwanda-speaking population of longer standing was mainly Hutu—unlike the mainly Tutsi influx of 1959—it split the Kinyarwanda-speaking minority into two hostile camps, Hutu and Tutsi, the Hutu fearful of once again coming under Tutsi rule.

To many in Kivu Province, the 1972 Citizenship Decree has come to symbolize not simply an inclusive citizenship policy but one so undiscriminating that, if followed in practice, it would surely turn Kivu into an open sanctuary for the surplus population from Rwanda and Burundi. 'What can't be accepted', a prominent civil society leader told us, 'is an order whereby every immigrant who comes is granted citizenship automatically—a practice that came in with Bisengimana becoming Chief of Staff to Mobutu'. Their anxiety fed by the provision in the 1972 Decree extending citizenship to 1959-60 refugees, the 'indigenous' majority—along with the Hutu amongst the Kinyarwanda-speaking minority—responded by demanding that the Tutsi in North and South Kivu be sent off to Rwanda.

The 1981 Citizenship Law: It is not until the legislative elections of 1977 that the 'indigenous' majority developed a strategy equal to countering the minority strategy of penetrating the security and party apparatus of the Mobutist party-state. The election brought home the realization that sheer numbers could be translated into political power, so that the majority could get access to power even if it was shut out of appointments in the state-party, the *Mouvement populaire de la révolution* (MPR). The 'indigenous' majority followed a single guideline: better not elect another Tutsi if you want to balance out against them. When one was elected—as was Gisaru, a Munyamulenge, as deputy of Uvira in South Kivu—the response of the local majority was to accuse him of having manipulated the election. Not surprisingly, the parliament that came out of the 1977 elections passed a new citizenship law. The 1981 law stipulated that only those persons who could demonstrate an ancestral connection to the population residing in 1885 in the territory then demarcated as Congo would qualify to be citizens of Congo.

It was one thing to pass the law, quite another to implement it. By the time of the 1985 provincial assembly elections, the question of citizenship was still unsettled, though the 1981 law remained on the books. In this context, the 'indigenous' majority improvised a solution: the Kinyarwanda-speaking population may vote in the elections, but none of its members may run for office. The solution seemed to compound the problem; for the fist time, all Kinyarwanda-speaking minority, particularly the Tutsi, was to smash ballot boxes. The result was that no provincial assemblies were elected in North or South Kivu.

The Sovereign National Conference (CNS) and the Resolution on Citizenship, 1991–92

The CNS took place at a time when the Banyarwanda minority was once again gripped by anxiety about their citizenship status. Following the Rwandan Patriotic Frint (RPF) attack on Rwanda in October 1990, many young Tutsi in Kivu decided to cross the border into Uganda and join the RPF. The Mobutu regime responded with a *Mission d'identification de Zairois au Kivu*, authorized to carry out an on-the-ground verification of who amongst the Kinyarwanda-speakers was Zairois and who was not— because their families had come after the Berlin Conference. As a result, many Hutu and Tutsi from 1936 were not verified as Zairois. This outcome in turn increased the flow of Tutsi youth crossing into Uganda to join the RPF.

By the time the Sovereign National Conference (CNS) met in 1991, citizenship had become a hot issue, particularly in the region of Kivu. Not surprisingly, the delegations from North and South Kivu urged the Sovereign National Conference to give priority to the citizenship issue. In response, the *Haut Conseil de la République*, an organ of the CNS, adopted the 1981 Citizenship Law.

The Sovereign National Conference marked a turning point in the political history of post-colonial Congo. This was so for at least two reasons. Countrywide, the CNS heralded the coming together of an internal peaceful opposition to the Mobutist party-state. In Kivu, however, it had a double significance: it also marked an important step in the constitution of a self-conscious political majority. This majority transcended ethnic lines and saw itself as an 'indigenous' majority threatened by a 'non-indigenous' minority growing through the periodic influx of refugees.

To understand why a majority constituted through the democratic process would appear as a threat to the minority, we need to take a brief look at the history of the internal opposition. The history of organized peaceful opposition goes back to the formation of the *Union pour la démocratie et le progress social* (UPDS) in 1982. This formation was the result of several impulses, including calls for reform from thirteen Parliamentarians in 1980. Whereas the tendency before 1980 was for opponents of the regime to flee into exile, the tendency after 1980 favoured the growth of a peaceful internal opposition to the regime. It is the gradual development of this internal opposition, in a favourable international context marked by the reform wave that followed the end of the Cold War, that led to Mobutu's 'opening up' speech of April 24, 1990. In that speech, he promised political reform. As a first step, Mobutu promised to relinquish the presidency of the MPR, and thereby ensure the separation of the party and the state. In the two weeks before he took that promise back, the idea of holding a Sovereign National Conference had caught the imagination of the political opposition. The CNS opened officially on 7 August 1991.

The proceedings of the CNS were televised throughout urban Congo. This was enough to inspire further initiatives. There was a mushrooming of civil society organizations, thickening the texture of the internal political opposition. We shall take two examples from the city of Kisangani to illustrate this tendency. The first relates to a socio-cultural centre formed in 1987 by a number of the city's college-educated youth in response to the ruling party's attempt to monopolize cultural activities for young people. The focal point of the centre's cultural activities was to 'denounce injustice through theatre'. But the centre had found it difficult to work openly. This changed with the CNS. When the CNS was suspended in 1992, members of the centre joined other youth in public protest. Many were arrested. That provided the impulse for further organization: members of the centre created *Les amis de Nelson Mandela* as a human rights organization on October 6, 1992, and launched a publication, *Liberté*. 'We felt in the National Conference we had found the medium of our emancipation', concluded one of the youthful organizers of *Les amis*.

Another group that followed in the wake of the CNS was *Groupe Lotus, ONG des Droits de l'homme et de développement*. The president of the group explained the circumstances of its formation in April 1992:

> Many of us used to meet from 1991 to discuss what was going on in the country. Then, we would meet at the parish meeting hall. The population of Kisangani and surrounding areas had very little idea of their rights. The other characteristic peculiar of Kisangani was a wait and see attitude, that problems will somehow be solved from the outside. This was reinforced by the fact that while people were following the Sovereign National Conference on television, few had any idea of what it was all about. This is how the Lotus Group was born. There were twelve of us and we decided to call ourselves LOTUS. We wanted to convey the idea of unity of diversity by reference to the flower lotus—since we came from many different environments. There was a biologist amongst us whose thesis

supervisor was from India and who suggested that in Indian culture, whenever there is disagreement and difference, they bring out the Lotus flower!

Like many other civil society organizations, the Lotus Group concentrated on recruiting from amongst the educated youth. They concentrated on recruiting those young people above the age of 21 with a secondary education at the minimum. Their activities were carried out in Kiswahili and Lingala. Once a member was accepted, they would go through a training workshop, focusing on both the objectives of the group and a social analysis of Congo, with a specific emphasis on human rights issues. The group had political scientists, medical doctors, and economists amongst its members, but not lawyers and jurists, who tended to gravitate to *Les amis*. Their activities were mainly around publications, lobbying and concrete support to people whose rights had been violated. Anyone approaching the group with a rights violation would be assigned two individuals to accompany them through all legal and related procedures.

The overall thrust of the CNS was to deepen and to coordinate the internal opposition to the Mobutist state. At the same time, the CNS impacted on the provinces in different ways. In the region of Kivu, it tended to crystallize two related trends: one in the 'indigenous' majority, the other in the Kinyarwanda-speaking minority. It accelerated the majority tendency to lump together all Tutsi, regardless of the depth of their presence on Congolese soil, into a single group. The tendency to use the term Banyamulenge as a generic term for all Congolese Tutsi really gathered momentum with the CNS. Correspondingly, it was during the CNS that the Banyamulenge found out that, their expectations to the contrary, their situation was not very different from that of the Tutsi of North Kivu.

The Sovereign National Conference brought two contradictory political tendencies to a head in Kivu. While the Kinyarwanda-speaking minority—particularly the Tutsi—continued to look to organs of the state-party, including its security organs, for protection against the 'indigenous' majority, the majority continued to invest in representative processes both as protection from the arbitrary rule of the party-state, and as guarantee that they would prevail against the minority. The very democracy that tended to create a majority across ethnic lines, tended to pit a self-consciously 'indigenous' and Congolese majority against what many increasingly came to think of as a 'non-indigenous' minority that was not only Kinyarwanda-speaking but also owed political allegiance to Rwanda. This is why it should not be surprising that the very fact that the CNS began to discuss the question of citizenship raised a fear in the minority that it was about to lose its citizenship.

When we talked to civil society leaders in Kivu in September 1996, we found that the citizenship of the Kinyarwanda-speaking minority was still a matter of debate amongst them. Who should be a citizen and who should not. Should the Mobutu/Bisengimana Decree of 1972, allowing all refugees of 1959 to become Congolese citizens, prevail? Or should there be an affirmation of the 1981 law passed by parliament and affirmed a decade later by the Sovereign National Conference, that only those with a proven connection to an ancestor resident in the territory demarcated as Congo in 1885 be verified as Congolese? Or should all those currently resident in Congo, who pledge political allegiance exclusively to the Congolese state, be considered Congolese—regardless of their parentage, place of birth or duration of stay in Congo? We found all these views present in the leadership of civil society, with a lively debate amongst them.

At the end of the discussions, we were left with two strong conclusions. The first related to civic citizenship, the second to ethnic citizenship. The more we pressed home the link between the mounting political crisis in Kivu and the citizenship question, the more those we spoke to tended to agree that the more inclusive option may also be the most prudent. The other side to this growing consensus—that all those resident in Congo before the Rwanda Genocide of 1994 be recognized as its citizens—was an equally firm consensus that ethnic citizenship must be restricted only to 'indigenous' Congolese. While the first tendency was a source of hope, the second gives real insight into the crisis of citizenship in contemporary Kivu.

The Crisis of Ethnic Citizenship

The institutional underpinning of ethnic identity is the Native Authority. Ethnic identity in the colonial state went alongside a batch of rights, best thought of as group rights since they could not be accessed except through the membership of an ethnic group. Since only those ethnic groups officially classified as indigenous had the right to a full-fledged Native Authority of their own, the 'customary' rights associated with the membership of a Native Authority were also exclusively the privilege of those considered 'indigenous'. To understand why 'non-indigenous' citizens in rural areas should persistently call for a Native Authority of their own, we need to begin with a fuller understanding of the Native Authority in Kivu.

The Native Authority in Kivu is three-tiered. At the lowest level is the chief of the locality. Then comes the second level chief, the *Chef de groupement*, and then finally the Mwami of the *Collectivité*. Those considered non-indigenous and living in rural areas may, and usually do, have a chief of the lowest order from amongst their own ranks, one who is answerable to the higher authority for their immediate governance. Only those considered indigenous, however, have the right to a chief of the second and third tier from one of their own. The distinction is crucial for customary power really rests at the level of the *Chef de groupement* and the Mwami. They have the power to confirm ethnic belonging and issue identity cards, oversee administration, allocate customary land for livelihood, hold tribunals through which customary justice is meted out, run local markets, and so on.

To understand the growing dilemma of the Rwandese-speaking minority in Kivu, we need to understand their changing relationship to the Native Authority system. The Rwandese-speaking minority consists of three territorially distinct groups, the Banyaruchuru and the Banyamasisi in North Kivu, and the Banyamulenge in South Kivu. As we shall see, the Banyaruchuru and the Banyamasisi are predominantly Hutu, whereas the Banyamulenge are Tutsi. Furthermore, the Hutu of Ruchuru are considered 'indigenous', and so are entitled to a Native Authority of their own. The Hutu of Masisi have also claimed an 'indigenous' status. Though it has been officially upheld some times, this claim has been hotly disputed at all times by other ethnic groups in North Kivu. The Tutsi of Mulenge, in contrast, have never managed to get their own Native Authority.

North Kivu: The Banyaruchuru and the Banyamasisi

The Rwandese-speaking population in North Kivu can be divided into three major groups from a historical point of view. Only one of these, the Banyarwanda of the part of Ruchuru called Bwisha, was present in the province before colonialism. Bwisha was a part of the pre-colonial Rwandan Kingdom. Before colonialism, it was governed by a Tutsi chief who paid homage to the Mwami in the Central Kingdom. When colonial frontiers were consolidated in 1918, and Bwisha made a part of Congo, Belgian colonialism replaced the Tutsi chief with a Hutu, Daniel Ndeze. The Rwandese-speaking population of Bwisha have thus always been considered indigenous, and have had a Native Authority of their own. The point of conflict in Bwisha has been whether that authority should be Tutsi (as before 1918) or Hutu (as after 1918).

In 1933, Belgians set up an authority to facilitate the immigration of labour from Rwanda into North Kivu. The *Mission d'immigration de Banyarwanda* was active until 1957. Banyarwanda immigrants began to arrive in North Kivu, in Ruchuru and Masisi, from 1936 onwards. The 1936 influx laid the basis of a major conflict. The local population was opposed to the influx because they saw it as competition for land. Local chiefs, on the other hand, were happy to see more numbers coming in: given that ethnic strangers would have to give the chief an extra payment in return for the temporary right to use land, every new immigrant meant an additional source of tribute. To escape that very tribute, the 1936 immigrants insisted on having their own Native Authority. In response to this demand, Belgian power cut off a part of the Hunde chefship, called it *Collectivité Gishari*, and put it under a Rwandese-speaking chief. Even though the 1936 immigrants were mainly Hutu, Belgium appointed a Tutsi as chief of Gishari.

The third group of Banyarwanda in North Kivu comprise the second wave of immigrants, those who fled Rwanda in the aftermath of the 1959 'social' revolution. Whereas both the pre-1918 residents of Bwisha and the 1936 immigrants were mainly Hutu, the 1959–60 influx was mostly Tutsi.

The social composition of the immigrants and the nature of Belgian colonial policy combined to create a double grievance—giving rise to a double tension. The source of the first tension was the tendency for the relationship between Hutu and Tutsi to get posed here as in Rwanda. As the tension between Hutu and Tutsi increased in Rwanda, so it did in North Kivu. This is clear from the impact of the 1959 'social' revolution in Rwanda. As the group that came in 1959–60 began to organize to return to power in Rwanda, relations began to sour, both with the 'indigenous' majority, and between Hutu and Tutsi in the Kinyarwanda-speaking minority.

The second source of tension was the relationship between the local population, the Bahunde, and Banyarwanda immigrants as a whole. The more the Bahunde saw the creation of a Banyarwanda Native Authority (*Collectivité Gishari*) as a violation of their 'customary' right, the more they mounted protest against it. In response, the Belgians decided to suppress Collectivité Gishari as a Banyarwanda Native Authority and to return former Bahunde chiefs to the area. To understand the explosive impact of this decision, we have to consider how rapidly the local situation had changed over the decades. To begin with, the *Mission d'immigration* had decided to bring immigrants to Masisi precisely because it was a low-density area where it would be easy for immigrants to access land. For this very reason, the immigration also led to a steady trickle of infiltrators who tended to come and settle next to those who had been neighbours in Rwanda. Unable to get free access to land, they tried to purchase it. This mode of settlement and accumulation had a double result. One, the Banyarwanda immigrants came to comprise a majority of the local population by the time of independence; two, it is these immigrants who had tilled and valorised most of the land in Masisi. Since many of the Banyarwanda had acquired land by purchasing it through the market, they considered it their private property. Yet, the Bahunde chiefs expected tribute from immigrants using land without a 'customary' right to it. Congo became independent with this poisoned legacy. The first major conflict between the Kinyarwanda-speaking population and those considered indigenous, known as *La guerre du Kinyarwanda*, broke out in 1963. This conflict lasted two years.

For the two decades that stretched from the end of La guerre du Kinyarwanda to the citizenship law of 1981—which reversed the 1972 decree linked to Mobutu/Bisengimana and which extended citizenship to refugees of 1959–60—the nationality conflict in North Kivu revolved around two pivots. The first pitted the 'indigenous' majority against the Kinyarwanda-speaking minority, whether immigrant or not. The more this tension grew the more it tended to blur all historical distinctions between different groups of Banyarwanda: distinctions between immigrants and non-immigrants, and between different groups that had immigrated at different times. As a consequence, all Kinyarwanda-speakers came to be considered non-indigenous. The second pivot of conflict was internal to the Banyarwanda; it pit the Tutsi against the Hutu. When articulated with the first, there was a tendency for the Hutu, who had either been there before the colonial period or came during its heyday, to claim an indigenous status against the Tutsi, most of whom arrived in North Kivu after 1959.

The shift from a mainly Banyarwanda immigrant identity, to an identity highlighting the difference between Hutu and Tutsi, is reflected in the breakup of *Umoja*, a common Banyarwanda organization, into two separate bodies, one Hutu, the other Tutsi, in the 1980s. Umoja was formed as a joint Hutu/Tutsi organization in the aftermath of the 1981 Citizenship Law which classified as non-citizen all Banyarwanda who came to Congo after its colonial boundaries were drawn up in 1885. We talked to its second President, Senzeyi Ryamukuru. He claimed that Umoja was formed at the behest of the first president of the Provincial Assembly of Kivu, Bisukero. After consultation between Bisukero and Ryamukuru, two young men, one Hutu (Sekimonyo Cosmos) and the other Tutsi (Munyamakuo David) were given the task of bringing local Hutu and Tutsi together in a single organization. Umoja was born as an organisation of all Congolese Hutu and Tutsi from Goma, Ruchuru and Masisi. Sekimonyo became its first president in 1983. In 1985, Sekimonyo (Hutu) became the president of the Regional Assembly, and Ryamukuru (Tutsi) became president of Umoja. In another few years, however, Umoja was no more.

Umoja disintegrated in 1988 and was replaced by separate Hutu and Tutsi organizations. It was with the direct financial support of Habyarimana and the political support of Mobutu that the Hutu in Ruchuru built links with the Hutu in Masisi and formed a common Hutu organisation called Maghrivi (*Mutuel des agriculture du Vironga*). It was said that part of Mobutu's electoral strategy was to identify 'indigenous' Hutu through Maghrivi so as to grant them citizenship. The main message of Maghrivi was that there are no 'indigenous' Tutsi in Congo. The proof, it was said, was the Native Authority, which was Hunde in Masisi and Hutu in Ruchuru. Maghrivi called for elections of all chiefs. It figured that an electoral strategy would both neutralize the Bahunde claim to be 'indigenous' and would translate the numerical majority of the Hutu into local political supremacy over both the Bahunde and the Tutsi. In response, Sekimonyo, a former president of Umoja, founded SIDER (*Syndicat d'initiative pour le développement de la zone Ruchuru*), as an exclusively Tutsi organization. SIDER was later absorbed into the ADP, the *Alliance démocratique du people*; the difference, according to Sekimonyo, was that ADP was an organization of all Congolese Tutsi.

South Kivu: The Barundi and the Banyamulenge

The minority question in South Kivu is less complex. Whereas the situation in North Kivu has a longer history and is intimately affected by what happens in Rwanda, the situation in South Kivu is of more recent origin but is influenced by developments in both Rwanda and Burundi.

Thus we find that the immigrant minority in South Kivu is from both Burundi and Rwanda.

Those living in South Kivu and Burundi have tended to shift back and forth between two adjacent valleys: Imbo Valley in Burundi and Ruzizi Valley in South Kivu. Today, the population of both valleys is Kirundi-speaking. Thus, the Kirundi-speaking population in South Kivu is considered 'indigenous' to the region. Like the Banyarwanda in Ruchuru in North Kivu, the Barundi in Ruzizi Valley have also had a customary chief of their own, in a *collectivité* named Barundi. Historically, the population in the *collectivité* has been Hutu but the chief Tutsi. This changed in 1994 when Mobutu decided to play with the Hutu; he replaced the Tutsi chief with a Hutu chief.

The Banyamulenge are mainly Tutsi. It is said that their arrival in South Kivu dates to the 1880s, when the central kingdom of Rwanda was ruled by Rwabugiri. Two explanations are advanced for the movement of Tutsi away from the kingdom. The first relates Rwabugiri's determination to gather more tribute from the rich, the second to the bitter conflict of succession that took place at his death, an event named after the place where he was buried to proclaim his successor. The result is a struggle for succession at the king's death. When the conflict is particularly bloody, those who lose are compelled to move away.

The claims about when and why the Banyamulenge moved are many and have multiplied as the political crisis has intensified. What I am recording here is the most coherent explanation we could get from historians sympathetic to the Banyamulenge predicament. After the original migration of the Banyamulenge—whether it took place during the reign of Rwabugiri or as an aftermath of the succession conflict at his death—there followed successive migrations. The next largest was that of Tutsi refugees in 1959-60. Unlike the bulk of the Banyamulenge who live on the high plains and are pastoralists, the 1959-60 refugees tend to live in urban areas or in refugee camps, such as Kalonge near the airport.

Unlike the Barundi, however, the Banyamulenge have never had a Native Authority of their own. Banyamulenge chiefs have been confined to the first level, the chief of the locality. For access to land, they had to pay homage to the existing chiefs wherever they settled. The area in which the Banyamulenge live covers three *territoires* (territorial administrations): (a) Mwenga inhabited by the Balega; (b) Fizi inhabited by the Babemba;and (c) Uvira inhabited by the Bavira and the Bafuliro. The *territoire* is a fourth level of *administration*, after the *localité*, the *groupement*, and the *collectivité*; it comprises several *collectivités*. The territoire of Uvira thus comprises three *collectivités*, called the Bavira, the Barundi and the Bafuliro. The name of each *collectivité* is taken from the name of the ethnic group considered 'indigenous' to it.

We can now see the location of the ethnic political problem. Whereas the 'customary' power—the power at the level of the *collectivité*—is defined mono-ethnically, the population resident on the ground is multi-ethnic. Thus, for example, while the power and the locality are defined as Bafuliro, the resident population includes both the 'indigenous' Bafuliro and the immigrants. These immigrants used to be known as Banyarwanda, or even as Batutsi, but now claim to be Banyamulenge, an identity that is highly contentious from the point of view of the Bafuliro. The Bafuliro point out that Mulenge is the name of the place, the *groupement* where the Tutsi were first allowed to settle by the Bafuliro. In 1924, they asked for permission from the colonial power to occupy the high plateau further south. When the permission was granted, they moved south—which is why some writers claim they arrived in 1924. The term may seem innocent on the surface but is not, claim the Bafuliro, for it really sums up the Tutsi claim to own Mulenge, which actually was owned by Bafuliro. The Bafuliro point out that the Tutsi have developed a tendency to call themselves by the name of the place where they have settled. Thus there are now Banya-tulambo, and Banya-minembwe, and so on.

We thus have two radically different types of identities: one tied to ethnic origin, the other to territory. Each makes sense if we realize that the identity in question is political, and that the point of political identity is to claim (or to deny) political rights. From the point of view of the immigrant ('non-indigenous') population, the fact that the power is identified in ethnic terms (Bafuliro) means that rights too are restricted to those who belong ethnically, in this instance to the Bafuliro, thereby disenfranchising all others. The claim to shift identity from the ethnic (the Banyarwanda) to the territorial (the Banyamulenge) must, in this context, be seen as an attempt to define a more inclusive basis of rights, being residence rather than ethnicity.

To 'indigenous' groups, however, the claim to a territorial identity appears as nothing less than subversive. All the 'indigenous' groups share the fear that the claim to a place-based identity really masks an immigrant strategy designed to lay claim to local land. Why else, many ask, would the

Banyamulenge seek to distinguish themselves from the Banyarwanda, except to erase their history, the fact that they came from Rwanda? The result, they point out, is that any Kinyarwanda-speaking person is free to follow the same strategy and claim to be a Munyamulenge, and thus a Congolese, no matter how brief their presence on Congolese soil.

We tried to explore the historical context in which the term Banyamulenge came to be of use. Some historians we spoke to in South Kivu said the triggering event was really the 1972 genocide of Hutu in Burundi, after which the Tutsi became very unpopular in the whole area. Though the term was in use earlier and came to be in greater use after the elections of 1977, the Banyarwanda in South Kivu really began to distance themselves from Rwanda after the genocide of 1972 in Burundi. What was for the Congolese Tutsi a way of distancing themselves from the socially explosive world of the Hutu and the Tutsi in Rwanda and Burundi became for the 'indigenous' Congolese a way for immigrants to disguise their real identity! At the same time, we have seen that this contention also has a significance from the point of view of the citizenship question. For the difference between these two types of political identities—one territorial, the other ethnic—is also an opposition between two contrasting ways of laying a claim to rights.

Rwanda and Kivu Province

Conventional wisdom in Goma and Bukavu has it that Kivu Province is where losers in Rwanda traditionally end up; and it is from Kivu that they prepare to return to power in Rwanda. A civil society activist in Bukavu explained the long-term effect of Rwandese conflicts that end to 'spill over into our country':

> These ethnic conflicts are cyclic with each ethnic group taking turn in power and misfortune. The fate of one today is the fate of the other tomorrow. The consequence for us are the refugees of the conflict. Another consequence of cyclical fortunes is that when they return, not everyone returns, some remain. Those who remain become Congolese.

The escalating crisis in Rwanda has introduced a double tension in Kivu, both external and internal, both a tension between Kivu and the power in Rwanda and a tension within Kivu society. This tension has tended to grow in intensity as the Rwandese-speaking refugees and exile population in Kivu has grown in size, increasing the weight of refugees and exiles while blurring the distinction between them and earlier immigrants. This has, in turn, fed the tendency on the part of many 'indigenous' Congolese to refuse to distinguish between Rwandese-speaking and refugees and exiles from Rwanda. In the aftermath of the genocide of 1994 in Rwanda, however, the effect has been like that of importing a deadly virus into the body politic of Kivu, and eventually Congo. To understand the impact of the two million plus refugees who streamed into North and South Kivu from post-genocide Rwanda, we need to sketch the contours of ethnic relations in North and South Kivu on the eve of the genocide.

The numbers of Kinyarwanda-speaking people in Kivu province exploded with the genocide of 1994 in Rwanda, as over two million refugees streamed into North and South Kivu. In North Kivu, in particular, their arrival coincided with a rapidly escalating ethnic conflict. To understand fully their impact on the situation in the region of Kivu, we need to bear in mind that the refugee question actually mediated a relationship between three different factors. These were: the local conflict in Kivu; the explosive dynamic of the Hutu/Tutsi conflict in Rwanda; and the pernicious role of major foreign powers, particularly France and the UN.

The ethnic conflict in North Kivu was triggered by a land conflict. This conflict did not pit one ethnic group against another, but poor Hutu against rich Hutu. To understand the relationship between class conflict within an ethnic group and the conflict between ethnic groups, one needs to recognize that there are actually two ways of acquiring land under the system inherited from colonialism. One is through a market transaction, a way that by its very nature is open only to the well off, those with means to register a preference on the market. The other is by asserting one's 'customary' right as a member of a Native Authority. This more political way is the only one open to the poor.

The land conflict in North Kivu began in Masisi in 1993, as a class conflict amongst the Bahutu, and then turned into an ethnic conflict between the Bahutu and the Bahunde over whether the former should have the right to their own Native Authority. At the outset, the Batutsi joined the 'indigenous' Bahunde (and the Banyanga) against the Bahutu. By the end of the year, however, as the conflict came to focus on the question of who was entitled to customary rights to land through a customary authority, it pitted the 'indigenous' (the Bahunde and the Banyanga) against the 'non-indigenous' (the Bahutu and the Batutsi).

Masisi is an area with a Hutu immigrant majority, said to be around 75 per cent of the local population by the early 1990s. The conflict began when rich absentee Bahutu (and some Batutsi) landlords began taking over the lands of mostly poor Bahutu (and some Bahunde) in Masisi. The displaced poor, said to be around 1000, fled to Walikali where they demanded the right to elect their own ethnic leaders. Since the Wanyanga held that this 'customary' right could only be exercised by those indigenous to the soil, the claim led to a clash between the Bahutu 1000 and the Wanyanga in Walikali. The poor 1000 then returned to Masisi, where they made the same 'democratic' claim, except that this time they also had the backing of their richer kin, the rich Hutu, and the general Kinyarwanda-speaking population. The claim led to a conflict with the Bahunde in Masisi. According to the leaders of the civil society–based Peace Campaign in Goma, the emerging Bahutu point of view was strongly shaped by the Hutu organization Maghrivi, itself influenced strongly by the ideological leadership provided by President Habyarimana in Kigali. Habyarimana, it seems, had by then come to consider himself as the president of all Bahutu, globally.

The response of the Mobutist state to growing conflict in Masisi was to send in units of the DSP and the *Garde civile*, neither, however, were provided with means of sustenance. All were forced to live off the local population, which they did. The difference was that while the DSP lived off the more prosperous Bahutu, the *Garde civile* lived off both the Bahunde and the ordinary Bahutu! The result was that the army ended up protecting the land claims of the 'non-indigenous' (mainly the Bahutu) against the 'indigenous' (mainly the Bahunde) population, while the conflict grew into a bloody affair. When we asked a Xaverienne Father in Bukavu to give us an idea of the intensity of the conflict, he estimated that between 10,000 and 20,000 were killed, while some 200,000 Bahunde, Bahutu and Batutsi must have run away in the process.

This was the context in which two-million-plus refugees streamed from Rwanda into North and South Kivu. The first set of refugees actually came in from Burundi into South Kivu in late 1993 and early 1994. These were mainly Bahutu fleeing the terror of the army after the assassination of Ndadaye in October. They numbered roughly 50,000 and were unarmed. The second influx of the Bahutu from Rwanda proved overwhelming for two reasons.

First, Hutu refugees numbered over two million. Secondly, they lived in armed camps, controlled by the ex-FAR and the *Interahamwe*, who continued to be supplied militarily by the French. The armed soldiers and militia were said to number some 20,000 in Bukavu and 30 to 40,000 in Goma. According to a local priest working with the Catholic Relief Services (Caritas) in Bukavu, there was agreement between the French and Mobutu that the soldiers of the Habyarimana state would not be disarmed by the Congolese army. The refugee question allowed Mobutu to resurface politically by posing as the protector of refugees in central Africa.

Both the UN system and US-based NGOs, however, continued to treat these armed camps as exclusively refugee settlements. Along with mainly American-funded international NGOs, the United Nations High Commissioner for Refugees (UNHCR) continued to provide daily provisions for the inhabitants of these camps, advertising this as a humane and charitable act. We asked the Congolese priest who worked with Caritas, also the local partner of UNHCR in providing assistance to refugees, who he thought bore moral responsibility for that situation. His answer was categorical. The responsibility lay with UNHCR since it had a real choice in late 1994. That choice was to ask member states to disarm the camps so as not to have to feed what was fast turning into an army. The contrast with Tanzania, which had to shoulder the burden of a million plus refugees, should make this clear. Unlike Tanzania, which had a functioning central state and army, Zaire did not. In the absence of a functioning central state in Mobutu's Zaire, it was clear that only the international community was in a position to impose a solution on Mobutu.

It is from this point of view that the larger responsibility lay with France and with the UN. The French had deliberately and effectively used humanitarianism as a cloak for the defense of narrow state interests. Through *Operation Turquoise*, France had gone out of its way to create a protective corridor to save those politically responsible for the genocide in Rwanda. The UN had watched the unfolding of the genocide in Rwanda without so much as lifting a finger. In similar fashion, they watched with complacency both the establishment of refugee camps in the vicinity of international borders, and the arming and training of refugees within these camps.

The setting up of armed camps of Bahutu refugees made life hell for the Tutsi in North and South Kivu. Let us recall that, the threat of being declared non-citizens by the 1991 *Mission d'identification de Zairois au*

Kivu, had increased the cross-border movement of young Congolese Tutsi going to join the RPF for training. This movement lent credibility to the notion spread by some 'indigenous' organizations, including *Maghrivi*, that the Congolese Tutsi were really Rwandese, not just culturally but also in their political allegiance. Yet, the vast majority of Congolese Tutsi had stayed behind in spite of the bloody fighting in Masisi in North Kivu, for the simple reason they had everything to lose and little to gain by moving. That period came to an end in 1994. On the one hand, the Tutsi of Kivu felt physically endangered by the influx of over two million Hutu in armed camps; on the other, they felt a vacuum in Rwanda, to which they could retreat in safety. Even then, not all left willingly. While the 1959 refugees hoped to re-acquire their properties upon return, earlier immigrants had little desire to return to Rwanda, which held hardly any promise for them. When they left, they did so only because they felt they had to, simply because everyone seemed to want them to leave.

As if to underline this development, the High Command of the Republic—the Parliament of transition—sent a Member of Parliament, Mambweni Vangu, to review the situation in Kivu following the genocide of 1994. The Vangu Commission was stacked with anti-Banyarwanda extremists. All Kinyarwanda-speaking people, Hutu or Tutsi, are like refugees and must return home—such was the verdict of the Commission. The chorus was picked up by Anzulani Mbembe, the co-speaker of Parliament.

The situation in North Kivu reached a climax between March and May 1996, when the remaining Tutsi from Masisi and Ruchuru were identified and taken to the border. They were chased out, not killed. They moved into the Rwandan border town of Gisenyi, into refugee camps for Congolese Tutsi. In these same camps, one also found the Bahude, because the Bahutu had decided to go after all their historical enemies: the Banyanga, the Batutsi, the Bahunde. This was the peak of the crisis. It is also when the First Rebellion broke out, leading to the end of the Mobutu regime.

In contrast, the citizenship problem in South Kivu seemed forced until the 1994 refugees came in. Only then did the local administration begin to appropriate Tutsi property in the valley, openly supported by Anzuluni Mbembe, the co-speaker of Parliament. Under pressure from armed Bahutu in the camps and from soldiers of the Congolese army, the Banyamulenge began to forge links with the RPF to acquire arms. Many in the valley population blamed Gapangwa, the Bishop of Uvira, for colluding in the arming of the Banyamulenge population. A similar split occurred in the Protestant Church, and even in the NGO population. An academic sympathetic to the plight of the Banyamulenge recalled that period, 'for anybody in the NGO world, to be publicly sympathetic to the Banyamulenge was to court death. The rationale was: how can you sympathize with those arming when the opposition is unarmed?' The reference to being unarmed was to the Congolese opposition, not to the Interahamwe in the armed refugee camps, nor to the Congolese army.

The insertion of two-million-plus refugees in camps that were armed and resourced from the outside had a devastating effect on civilian life in Kivu. First, it led to the dollarization of the economy. This bitter truth is best conveyed in the words of the Bukavu-based priest who participated in this humanitarian effort. 'One talks of all the humanitarian organizations that came here but one doesn't talk of all how they ruined our economy through its dollarization, its rents going up, local Zairois finding life increasingly beyond their reach. In short, amazing resources were deployed in an unreachable endeavour, one which did not correspond to our vision'. To talk to civil society leaders in Kivu about the experience of hosting two million plus refugees resourced through international NGOs is to listen to a litany of troubles—criminality, ill health, increased prices, lowered production, mounting insecurity—all traced to that single experience.

The second effect of armed refugee camps was to accelerate the tendency to militarize ordinary life. This happened in two inter-connected waves. The first was the result of the Hutu/Tutsi antagonism in Rwanda brought to a volcanic eruption by the 1994 genocide. Subject to a regime of terror unleashed by the Interahamwe in armed camps, more and more Congolese Tutsi crossed the border into Rwanda. In response, the RPF trained and armed the Congolese Tutsi. The second wave was internal to Kivu Province, where the Interahamwe roamed the countryside, often collaborating with the Congolese army. In response, many of the Native Authorities create their own militia. The anatomy of political life in Kivu began to resemble that in Rwanda. As in Rwanda, where every political party had come to have its own militia by the Genocide of 1994, so in Kivu every Native Authority began to acquire its own militia in the post-Genocide period.

The origin of the militia lie in the land conflict of 1993-94. The first militia were created by the 'indigenous' population in North Kivu as protection against the army when it entered the region and sided with the more prosperous Hutu. Faced with an 'indigenous' militia, the Hutu developed their own counter-militia, called *Les combattants*. After 1994, it collaborated freely with the Interahamwe. In a parallel movement, the Tutsi, concentrated in South Kivu, consolidated their organizations under a single umbrella, the *Alliance démocratique des peuples*, in November 1996. The ADP, as already pointed out, was an organization of the Congolese Tutsi.

While the biggest of the militia in Kivu were those of the Congolese Hutu and Tutsi, we were able to identify at least four militia organized on an 'indigenous' basis, all in North Kivu. The first of these, the Mayi Mayi,[2] was said to be based in the central area of Masisi and Walikale. Its recruits came mainly from two ethnic groups, the Bahunde and the Batembo. The second was the Ngilima. Based in the northern areas of Lubero and Beni, it drew members mainly from the Banande. The Banande were also the main force in the third militia, the Kasingien. The difference was that the Kasingien was a cross-border militia, its members coming from Congolese living on both sides of the Uganda-Congo border. With its headquarters at the foot of Mt. Ruwenzori, the Kasingien freely cooperated with the Ngilima. Like the Ngilima, the Kasingien also claimed to have found a mystical antidote that would render humans safe against bullets. The last militia we were told of is the Katuko. Operating in the area stretching from Kale in the south to Walikale in the north, its recruits were said to be mainly young Banyanga.

Just as the term *Banyamulenge* has become a generic term for all Congolese Tutsi, so the term *Mayi Mayi* has become a generic term for all militia in Kivu Province linked to 'indigenous' Native Authorities. The reason why the Mayi Mayi joined the First Rebellion in Congo, the rebellion against Mobutu, but opposed the rebellion when it came to power, is simple. They joined it when the rebellion targeted the Interahamwe and the allied Congolese army. And they opposed the rebellion when they saw it turn into the spearhead of what they feared was turning into a Rwandese occupation. This feeling was broadly shared amongst most civil society leaders we interviewed. We were constantly referred to two tendencies. The first was that the Rwandese army had turned into an army of occupation, the proof being that its commander was even formally appointed the

---

[2] *Maji* (pronounced *Mayi* in Kivu) means water in Kiswahili, possibly referring to the powers claimed for ritually-blessed water to render all those on whom it is sprinkled immune to the life-destroying effect of bullets.

commander of the Congolese National Army. Secondly, this army had begun to intervene directly in Congolese affairs, actively supporting demands by the Congolese Tutsi: that the Banyamulenge be given a separate Native Authority in South Kivu, and that the Hutu head of the Native Authority in Ruchuru (North Kivu) be replaced by a Tutsi, so as to return the situation to what it had been before 1918.

The ethnic situation in Kivu went from bad to worse with the success of the First Rebellion against Mobutu. The opportunity for removing a long-standing dictatorship in Kinshasa was turned into one for revenge seeking in Kivu. No sooner had the war begun than revenge killings started to happen in Goma (North Kivu). In the four months before our mission (September 1997), there were lots of killings—even more displaced people—particularly in Masisi as the Tutsi of North Kivu settled accounts with the Hutu in Maghrivi. A prominent civil society leader told us that approximately 6000 Hutu must have been killed in Goma alone in the short space of a week.

The situation in South Kivu was, if anything, worse. The 'Banyamulenge'—I put the term in quotes since we don't really know who these were—entered the Ruzizi Valley in September 1996. A prominent Bukavu-based intellectual, otherwise sympathetic to the citizenship claims of the Banyamulenge, described the situation to us in words that we would have dismissed as an exaggeration had they come from a stranger.

> The Banyamulenge conquered their rights by arms but the rift between them and the local population has grown. The attitude of the Tutsi soldiers—the Rwandese and the Banyamulenge—during and after the war has made them more detested by the population due to killings and torture. For example, they will go into the village, raid all the cattle, tell the population—since when have you learnt to keep cattle; we are cattle; we know cattle. In Bukavu, they went into and stole from houses. Not so much in Goma. The result is that the population is increasingly getting concerned over the question of the Tutsi presence.

Two tendencies seemed to be coming together in this assault on the 'indigenous' population. For the Congolese Tutsi, it seemed an opportunity to settle scores with local opponents. The Rwandese Tutsi, however, seemed to have generalized their hatred of the 'genocidaires', first to all Hutu, and then to the local population, seeing it as willing host to armed camps of the 'genocidaire'. But their actions fed wild fears in the local population. I recount some of these to give a sense of the incredibly tense situation that we encountered in Bukavu, more so than in Goma. Some thought that Tutsi power in Rwanda was trying to annex Kivu and turn it into a homeland for Bahutu. Others were convinced that a plan was afoot to kill the local 'indigenous' elite, such as intellectuals and business people, and that lists had already been compiled for the purpose. Several dates were in circulation. Bukavu seemed in a state of grand panic. 'Today', a highly respected academic assured us, 'it is being said that Ugandan and Rwandan soldiers are digging trenches all around the city, with guns aimed at the city. Everybody is preoccupied with security, not with how to improve relations with one another'.

Crisis tends to give rise to stereotypes and is in turn nourished by it. When we asked a peace activist in Goma to reflect on possible solutions to the conflict, he mused: 'One needs to ask the indigenous whether they can chase away all the Rwandese, and ask the Rwandese whether they can kill all the autochtone'. Unwittingly, he had given voice to popular stereotypes, reflecting popular fears: the Rwandese fear that they may be chased away by the 'indigenous', and the 'indigenous' fear that they may be killed by the Rwandese!

Militarisation spread two tendencies in Kivu and Congo, as it had in Rwanda. First, the link forged between militarization and genocidal tendencies inside Rwanda spread across its borders. The First Rebellion led to an indiscriminate slaughter of Interahamwe, of unarmed Hutu refugees, of the Hutu in Maghrivi, and even those Hutu not connected to Maghrivi. Those responsible for that slaughter became part of the post-Mobutu government, and were part of the forces that opposed a UN Inquiry into the matter. Though the Second Rebellion took place subsequent to our mission, it seems pertinent to note that those who carried out indiscriminate massacres of Hutu in Kivu are today a part of the military forces of the Second Rebellion. The Second Rebellion, in turn, evoked from the Kabila government an exhortation to the 'indigenous' population in Kivu to slaughter indiscriminately not only invading forces from Rwanda, but also the Congolese Banyamulenge in the rebellion, and even all Congolese Tutsi civilians. While Rwanda arms the Congolese Tutsi to beef up the Second Rebellion, the Kabila government arms Congolese Hutu as a counter measure. Each is determined to liquidate the other—physically. To keep this in mind is to beware that genocidal tendencies can no longer be equated with any particular ethnic group, or with just one side to the armed conflict in Congo.

The second effect of militarisation has been to reduce all credible politics to armed politics. The result is to marginalize all civil society-based politics. Once again, this tendency developed in a consolidated form in pre-genocide Rwanda where each political party felt compelled to organize its own militia, just to survive. In post-genocide Rwanda, there is both a tendency on the part of those in power to demonize all oppositional politics as 'genocidaire'—regardless of its political character—and a corresponding tendency on the part of all opposition to take on the character of armed opposition. In Congo, once again, the tendency to reduce all credible politics to armed politics can be found within both the Kabila government and the leadership of the Second Rebellion.

The Military Solution to Dictatorship

The Mobutist dictatorship gave rise to two different and often contradictory types of oppositions. One was internal and peaceful; the other was external and based on the use of violence. The internal process came to a head with the Sovereign National Conference, the external process with the march of the Rwandese army to dismantle military camps across Lake Kivu. The tension between the two processes remains at the heart of Congo's dilemma today.

The Sovereign National Conference opened officially on 7 August 1991 and was abruptly closed on 6 December 1992 when it was ready to deal with the two dossiers considered the most sensitive politically. These were the reports of the committee on ill-acquired goods and that on political assassinations. In spite of the fact that the CNS had won considerable public support, several activists insisted that its suspension should not just be seen as an indication of the regime's strength; the suspension, they argued, would not have been possible without the internal weakness of the opposition.

Some of the participants in the CNS told us that the internal weakness of the opposition should have been anticipated, and prepared for, since the population had been politically strapped for many years. At the same time, they felt the opposition had underestimated the capacity of the regime to learn that it could use that same freedom to advantage. We were given examples of how this was done with reference to the introduction of key freedoms, such as political party organization and women's participation in politics. When it came to the freedom to organize political parties, Mobutu decreed initially that only three parties would be registered. The restraint was lifted in response to popular pressure. The reform also gave room to those hoping to control the process by creating as many parties as possible. The MPR, the state-party, was the first to take advantage of this opportunity, creating several parties, both as a way of seizing the initiative and as a way of recycling itself. As the opposition discovered followers of MPR within its own ranks, it divided into two, the nominal and the radical opposition.

The MPR also took advantage of the weakness of women to reinstall their power, so much so that there were more women in the pro-MPR parties than in the actual opposition. Women leaders in civil society admitted that it took great courage for women activists to join the opposition, for it led to considerable isolation. Women in the MPR were treated as sexual objects. Whether young or old, all women were referred to as 'Maman MPR'. A woman leader explained to us that this way of using the word 'maman' (mother) for all women, whether married or not, was a way of abolishing all differences amongst women, so that all women—even the young children—could be treated as sexual objects. The point is that if you can call a 16-year old 'maman', then you are fixing her identity as a baby-making machine.[3]

Finally, the MPR was able to exploit the shallow history of oppositional politics to corrupt many of its leaders. The leaders who most openly accepted Mobutu's method of corruption ended up leaving the ranks of the opposition one by one. Yet, not all those who stayed remained untainted by these practices. Some in the ranks of the CNS linked even senior leaders to ill-acquired goods, and other questionable practices. Several agreed that the internal opposition was showing signs of floundering by the time the externally forged Alliance arrived on the scene. They attested to a general feeling that all that had been tried had failed, except the military option—why the population welcomed the military option when it was advanced by the First Rebellion.

The external process began with the march of the Rwanda army to dismantle militarized refugee camps across Lake Kivu. The ranks of the

---

[3] As if to underscore the point, the regime lowered the age of consent to 14. The adverse implications for the morale of the country's youth could not be missed by many. For that same reason, the National Conference raised the age of consent to 18.

Rwanda army included Congolese Tutsi irregulars—the Banyamulenge—who had earlier crossed the border into Rwanda to get military training from the RPF. Now, they were determined to press home a double claim, for a civic citizenship of Congolese state and for a Native Authority of their own in Kivu. The armed forces that gave the First Rebellion a military edge were predominantly Kinyarwanda-speaking, whether they came from Rwanda or from Kivu in Congo. It is this fact which led many, particularly in Kivu, to claim that the liberation was fast turning into an occupation.

By September 1997, disillusion had already set in with the new power. The leaders of civil society we spoke to were the most disenchanted with the new power. At the political level, the success of the anti-Mobutu rebellion had deepened the conflict between those who had carried out the war and those who had organized internally. They felt this conflict should not just be seen as a struggle for power, for it was also about the status of the internal opposition process. Stressing more the form of governance than the personality of governors, they decried the tendency of the new power to organize governance by starting from scratch rather than by taking into account the ideas adopted at the CNS. A civil society activist summed up this point of view: 'For a population that had become accustomed to a level of democratization, we find the new power working as a single party state unacceptable'.

At the socio-economic level, there was the question of the considerable wealth acquired by those from the old system. A lot of these properties had been seized as 'ill-acquired goods', but this was done without any juridical procedure. While the new power claimed these belonged to the state, the activists claimed they belonged to the new party, the AFDL. Socio-economic changes affecting the broader population—whether these related to the rate of exchange, the prices of goods, the imposition of new taxes or changes in old taxes, etc.—also seemed to be effected just as arbitrarily.

At the broad social level, there were latent conflicts that anyone with an interest in post-Mobutu Congo would need to keep in mind. The first was the tension between the East (including the city of Kisangani, though not the province as a whole) and the West. Overall, the old power around Mobutu was identified with the West, the new power around Kabila with the East. Linguistically, the West speaks Lingala, the East Kiswahili. The old power was using Kiswahili in the army and was trying to introduce it in the administration. The second tension is that between the 'indigenous' and the 'non-indigenous' in each province. The old power supported the 'indigenous' in every region. This way of doing things even had a name: it was called geo-politics. The new power, it was said, felt there should be no difference between the 'indigenous' and those from elsewhere.

We have seen that the most acute expression of this conflict was in Kivu, between those considered 'indigenous' and the Kinyarwanda-speaking minority. In the words of one of the leaders of the civic opposition:

> The position of Rwanda contributes to a sharp division within the country today, because Kabila got to power thanks to Rwandese support... President Kabila is a prisoner of the Rwandese people and now has great difficulty working with the internal opposition, because in this opposition there was a great deal of insistence on the resolutions of the Sovereign National Conference that posed the question of citizenship. Because of this, Rwanda continues to play a destabilizing role and contributes to the tension in the country.

At the state level, there were questions concerning both the continuing arbitrary way in which the state dealt with the civilian population, as illustrated by the number of abuses, gratuitous humiliations, beatings, torture and even killings without any procedure. At the same time, there was concern about the cleavages in the army. The army was seen as comprising two centres of privilege: on the one hand, the Tutsi (whether Rwandese or Congolese), and on the other, the Katangese from the region of the President. The rest, it was said, were left to fend for themselves. In hindsight, it would seem that it is the split between the two major centres of privilege in the post-Mobutu regime—the Tutsi and the Katangese, each with its set of regional backers—that has split the post-Mobutu power and ushered in the Second Rebellion.

In sum, the growing disillusion centred around two connected issues: national independence and democratic reform, the former external, the latter internal. Civic activists emphasized the relationship between them: Congo's independence, they argued, is a prerequisite for any sustainable internal reform. This point of view was succinctly articulated by one from Bukavu:

> The new power is seen as submissive to Rwanda and Uganda. Every decision it takes is seen as a dictation from outside. The problem is that democratization (if it is introduced now) would also be seen as an external imposition. So, democratization can only be a long-term solution, only after Kabila is seen as a Congolese power.

The Antidote to Militarism

We have traced the growth of two related tendencies: militarism, and the associated tendency for all organized politics to take on the form of armed politics. We have also sketched the dual context that nourished these tendencies: the land conflict that began in North Kivu in 1993 and turned into an armed ethnic conflict, and the transformation of camps of post-genocide refugees into armed camps in both North and South Kivu. It is the coming together of these two developments that explain the depth of the crisis in Kivu today. To identify the antidote to militarism, we need to begin with that same context.

It was local civil society in North Kivu, and not the state system controlled from Kinshasa, that tried to bring under control the land conflict that began in 1993 and turned into ethnic warfare over the years. The initiative came from the Goma-based Peace Campaign. Twice in November 1993 and once in February 1994, the Peace Campaign brought together the leaders of the warring factions for discussions. Concretely, this meant bringing some 250 warlords from the three warring groups in Masisi—the Bahunde, the Bahutu and the Batutsi—under a single roof. The initiative was remarkably successful in containing the conflict—until the massive influx of post-genocide refugees exploded tensions in Kivu.

The Goma-based Peace Campaign was overwhelmed as armed camps of a million plus refugees were set up in their backyard. It recovered as the First Rebellion cleared the armed refugee camps and displaced the Mobutu regime. Resuscitated with modest support from British NGOs, its activities ranged from radio broadcasts to conciliation teams that were multi-ethnic in composition, so they may negotiate every roadblock, be its authority Bahutu, Batutsi or Bahunde.

The Peace Campaign contributed to a civic culture of consultation and persuasion, as opposed to imposition, whether bureaucratic or military. That culture, in turn, had developed stronger roots in Kivu than the modest scope of the Peace Campaign's surviving activities would indicate. We came across evidence of this at various levels. While militarist tendencies had intensified within the state and ethnically-based organizations, it was clear that they were not yet hegemonic. They existed alongside parallel, and conflicting, tendencies. Two examples, one from the state sector and the other from ethnic society in Kivu, will illustrate the point. Both arose in response to growing ethnic conflict in Kivu.

The state response was said to be the outcome of a personal initiative by Bugera, the Secretary-General of the ADFL, himself a Tutsi who had come to North Kivu as a refugee in 1959. The Bugera initiative unfolded in July of 1997. By the time we got to Bukavu in September, it had blossomed into a government-sanctioned delegation called the Commission for Peace and Reconciliation in North and South Kivu. The group was composed and recomposed several times, usually following complaints that nominations included individuals who had made strong anti-Tutsi speeches under the previous regime. Finally, the Ministry of Internal Affairs formulated three criteria to guide the composition of the group: ethnic balance, not being directly implicated in the conflict, and minimum knowledge of the situation. The core of the team was put together in Kinshasa and comprised about 30 persons, including two from each ethnic group involved in the conflict, student observers, four from the Ministry and nominees of both the President and the Secretary-General of the Alliance. There were plans to expand it by incorporating a further ten through local nominations. We met with some of the members and with the Chairperson, a US-based Congolese conflict resolution expert.

The Chairperson's observations were of great interest for our mission. She told us that she had begun the mission by asking each member of the delegation to identify and prioritize three issues they considered critical for achieving peace in the region. At the top of the list was the question of power, that people in power are not 'indigenous' to area. She followed up with individual discussions, and explained the outcome.

> In this land, they can't say who are the real Congolese, who are refugees. They claim people in power are not true Congolese, that the whole army is made of Rwandese; they should go back. One issue is: how are we going to go for peace talks, so and so will poison us? This tribe is known for that. They said when we get to the Banyamulenge region we need to be careful what we eat. We need to be allowed to go and get our own food. When we had a group discussion, they did not come out with it. It comes out when I have discussions with individuals.

Local researchers in Goma were skeptical of the prospect of a peace delegation coming from Kinshasa-based political society. They contrasted the vantage point of those from political society unfavourably with that of researchers based in civil society.

> These are from political society and can not work well. The way of the politician is different from that of researchers. The main preoccupation of politicians is other calculations. So, when it is over, you are always brought back to the

situation as was before. On our side, we are working mostly with people who do want a solution but are not deeply involved in the conduct of the war. So, how they look at solutions is not fed by the emotional tie with the struggle.

That politicians have their limitations should not detract from the fact that there are different ways of doing politics with different consequences for the society at large. This fact was brought home to us in a discussion with the president of SIDER, one of the local warlords who had participated in the Peace Campaign discussions in 1993-94. When we asked him about his view of the situation, he said:

> The situation is worrying because there are antagonisms coming back to surface. The Mayi Mayi continue to say there are no people as Congolese Tutsi, and that Congo is increasingly being ruled by Tutsi.

But when we asked to suggest a solution to the incredibly tension-ridden situation in late 1997, he answered:

> If I was the government, I would organize a regional sovereign conference to allow everyone to express themselves, to say whatever they have against the other. This way all the complaints will come out and we will know what they are. Allow those fighting today to express themselves. This is the only way to deal with the situation.

His answer suggested that, in spite of the spread of militarist politics in the region, the Peace Campaign had not been in vain.

Summing up the Crisis

I have argued that the depth of the crisis in Kivu cannot be understood unless we see it as the result of a confluence of two distinct processes: the social crisis of post-genocide Rwanda and the citizenship crisis in Kivu. The genocide has given rise to a Zionist-type state in Rwanda. Two convictions underline the Zionist-type character of post-genocide power in Rwanda. The first is an overwhelming sense of moral responsibility for the very survival of all remaining Tutsi, globally. The result is that the post-genocide power is defined by a diasporic, rather than a territorial, notion of political obligation and political community. The second conviction—also a direct outcome of the experience of genocide—is that power is the condition of Tutsi survival. As the Congolese Tutsi legal advisor to the Secretary-General of the Alliance put it, 'In Rwanda, the Tutsi have reached a conclusion that power is the only guarantee for their right to life, otherwise they will be killed by Hutu'. The newly appointed Rwandese commander of the Congolese army echoed that same thought: 'The Tutsi are just a scared group, from 1959, 1973, 1994. They will feel no assurance until they are protected by Tutsi themselves. That is natural'.

I have defined the crisis of the region of Kivu as primarily a crisis of citizenship, in both its civic and ethnic dimension. Both aspects of the crisis have been exacerbated by the spillover of the Rwandese crisis into Kivu, dramatized by the flow of armed refugees and armed agents of the post-genocide state. When I asked the newly appointed Rwandese commander of the Congolese Army about how he intended to deal with local worries about who is a Kinyarwanda-speaking Congolese and who a Rwandese, his response was disarmingly simple:

> I have told them not to be bogged down by the imaginary borderline. Let peasants move freely. If we have peace, we should have free movement. Those who move will not be refugees, but migrants.

Later, we spoke to the legal advisor to the Secretary-General of the Alliance about how they intended to go about addressing Congolese Tutsi demands for a Native Authority of their own, in South and North Kivu. This person also happens to be the grandson of Mwami Nshizirungu, the Tutsi chief of Bwisha in Ruchuru until the Belgians demoted and replaced him in 1918 with Chief Ndeze, a Hutu. We asked the grandson about the implication of re-appointing Tutsi chiefs in Ruchuru, where the majority population is Hutu. His response, too, suggested he had yet to think through larger implications of policy reform: 'The chiefs that are being appointed now are the same chiefs who should have been there in 1920. They are just being reappointed'.

An adequate response to crisis needs to recognize its various dimensions and to disentangle them analytically—so as to formulate each separately in an overall research agenda. It is my strong recommendation that CODESRIA put together two separate initiatives, one on Rwanda and the other on Kivu (Congo). The Rwanda initiative needs to stress the volcanic nature of its internal crisis and the trauma that afflicts post-genocide Rwanda, and of the fact that the aftermath of this cannot be handled by the people of Rwanda, or even those of the region, on their own. Coming to terms with the trauma of the genocide must be defined as a global responsibility, as was the responsibility of coming to terms with the trauma of the Holocaust. The CODESRIA initiative needs to focus on two intersecting and tension-ridden relationships—between justice and democracy on the one hand, and justice and reconciliation on the other—and put these in a context that is at the same time local, regional and global. Because our mission did not directly focus on Rwanda, I cannot make any further recommendation beyond this general observation. My recommendations on Kivu follow a brief discussion of local research capacity.

Local Research Capacity

The infrastructure of university education in Democratic Republic of Congo developed around a core of state-funded universities.[4] First established in the three major cities of Kinshasa, Lumumbashi, and Kisangani, the state university system was later extended to Goma and Bukavu in Kivu Province. Though setup later, as a result of church and individual initiative, private universities now number ten and cover every province in the country. Even if this number is greater than that of state universities, private universities enroll a lesser number of students. By September, 1997, the time of our mission, the University of Kinshasa, with about 20,000 students, was the country's largest state university, and the Protestant University of Congo, with about 2,000 students, was its largest private university. We met with researchers in the state university system in Kinshasa, Kisangani and Kivu, and with those in the non-state system in North and South Kivu.

Today, the largest faculties at the University of Kinshasa are those of Medicine and Law. Each has approximately 5,000 students. While we were unable to get global figures on the gender composition of the student body, a first-year law student told us that 200 of the 500 students in his class were women. By 1995, all students were required to pay their fees in American dollars: Congolese nationals paid $100 for the first year, and $75 for each of the next two years, while foreign students paid a standard fee of $500 a year.

The university system in Kivu Province is divided between North Kivu (Goma) and South Kivu (Bukavu). Three institutions dominate the higher education initiative in Goma. Two of these—the Centre Université de Nord Kivu à Goma and University d'Etat du Goma—are state-funded, while the Protestant Université libre du pays de Grands Lacs is church-funded.

---

[4] Congo was the first country in Africa to boost a nuclear reactor for research purposes. Donated by the US Government to Lovanium University towards the end of the colonial period, it was an indication of the strategic importance with which the US would view an independent Congo.

Several autonomous initiatives have mushroomed around these institutions. Of particular interest to us was the Centre africain de recherche et d'éducation pour la paix (CAREP), also in Goma. CAREP was created specifically to think through the problems generated by the flood of post-genocide refugees from Rwanda into Kivu Province. Overwhelmed by a situation without precedent, a Doctor of Theology at the Université libre and a research fellow in the social sciences (also the Chief Academic Officer) at the Centre université decided to create a research NGO. They sought assistance from a Canadian professor, successfully. CAREP works with positive action groups whose focus is the building of peace. It does this mainly though holding workshops and publishing its reports. When we spoke to them in September 1997, CAREP hoped to hold a colloquium in March of 1998, comprising universities from around the Great Lakes—from North and South Kivu, Rwanda, and Burundi—along with others from Kinshasa, Kisangani, Lubumbashi, and a few from Uganda, Kenya and Tanzania. The object was to promote a sustained study of different factors involved in the expanding conflict in the Great Lakes.

The institutional base for research in contemporary Congo extends beyond the parameters of higher education to include research NGOs. Our brief experience leads us to the conclusion that most research NGOs are formed as a result of initiatives originating from the university system. To take two examples, the Vice Dean of Research at the Faculty of Social, Administrative and Political Sciences at the University of Kisangani is also the director of an NGO called Centre d'éducation populaire au droit de l'homme à la démocratie et au développement (CEPOD). Similarly, a member of the Faculty (also a doctor of theology) at the Université libre du pays des Grands Lacs was also the President of CAREP. While an NGO research sector has developed through academic initiative, this initiative should be seen as both a creative response to a rapidly spreading social crisis in the region, and a realistic accommodation to a rapidly changing donor agenda. In other words, these initiatives have fallen on fertile ground not only because the questions they raise resonate with widely shared concerns in different sectors of society, but also because donors have decided to commit resources to restructure civil society around a network of NGOs.

The donor cartel has clearly had a strong influence in shaping the NGO research agenda. We became aware of it every time we asked a person in the research community for a list of vital research issues. The answer inevitably sounded like a donor list—democratisation, human rights, gender, conflict prevention, etc.—so de-contextualised that it could have been presented to us almost anywhere in the world. We soon learnt that if we wanted responses sensitive to time and place, we had better begin with a discussion of the ongoing local situation and the unfolding crisis and only then put the question. The more we followed this practice, the more we were compelled to engage with our colleagues on issues of direct concern to them, rather than follow a routine procedure of recording answers to prepared questions. In the process, we too sharpened our perspective on the crisis and on what kind of research agenda would most adequately reflect its urgency. As I have already explained, subsequent events have made it difficult for us to continue to function as a team. The recommendations that follow are strictly my own.

Recommendations

My recommendation for a research agenda on Kivu (Congo) focus on the various aspects of the crisis of the state, and the antidote the crisis continues to generate, however feeble this may seem at the moment. These are followed by other recommendations on networking, academic support and publication support.

Proposed Research Agenda

i) State reform and the question of citizenship.
- The citizenship question and its two aspects: civic and ethnic.
- The rights of 'indigenous' people.
- Relation between central and local government: unitarism vs. Federalism.
- Comparative research on the reform of customary power.
- Comparative research on Banyarwanda immigrants in the Great Lakes regions: particularly, Uganda, Congo and Tanzania.

ii) Militarisation of politics, economy and society: tendencies and counter-tendencies.

iii) Relationship of civil to political society, with specific reference to the political role of civil society in times of crisis.

iv) Gender politics and the state: contradictions of participation and incorporation of women in state politics.

v) The land question and ethnic conflict.

vi) Informal economy and its relationship to day-to-day survival of the people vs. developmental contribution to gross domestic product.

Networking

CODESRIA needs to commit resources to network all research institutions, and particularly the research NGOs, into the wider CODESRIA family. The advantage of such an initiative will be three-fold. One, the new institutional members would individually contribute to a benefit from the wider pool of research experience in Congo, the region and the continent. Two, CODESRIA would liaise with and thus protect them from an eager—even if well-intentioned—donor cartel impatient to shape the research agenda on the ground. Finally, such a network will also introduce an institutionalized cooperation between universities and research NGOs. This will have the invaluable effect of countering the tendency for NGO-based research to be detached from university-based teaching.

Academic Support

- The networking of institutions should be accompanied by a programme that establishes an exchange of academics and researchers between institutions in the region. The University of Kisangani, for example, has only one full professor in the Faculty of Social, Administrative and Political Sciences. He is also the Dean of the Faculty. With 30 doctoral thesis projects registered this year, the Faculty is compelled to rely on the services of visiting professors, mainly from Kinshasa and Lubumbashi.

- CODESRIA should consider organizing support for initiatives (such as by CAREP) to organize thematic workshops that bring together researchers from different institutions in the region for joint deliberation on common concerns.

Publication Support

CODESRIA needs to give direct support to publish research results. We give three examples below.

- CAREP publishes yellow books, mainly a collection of workshop reports whose focus is the ideas people generate in the course of trying to live together. The pink books explain the methodology of how to work together in groups. These are mainly designed as manuals for training teachers. CAREP was working on six additional books in September 1997. These were:

    a) Poverty in North Kivu: its causes and consequences;
    b) The hidden war in North Kivu;
    c) The struggle to combat negative values;
    d) Tribalism: its forms and negative effects;
    e) Insecurity in North Kivu;
    f) Lack of popular education.

- Peace Campaign used to publish reports, with assistance from French sources, but is now short of resources.

- The Faculty of Social, Administrative and Political Sciences at the University of Kisangani has a research unit, L'Institut de recherche sociale appliquée (IRSA) which publishes a Revue de IRSA. The Revue had depended heavily on Belgian funding, which stopped in September 1992.

Appendix: List of Persons Interviewed

- Comrade Alec, Pan African Movement, Kinshasa
- Dr. Hamuli Kabaruza, Secretary-General, CRONGD, Kinshasa
- Mr. Steven Muzido, airline employee, Goma
- Mr. Mbusa Nyamwisi, Member from Butembo, North Kivu, Peace Commission for Kivu, Goma
- Dr. Collete Madishi-Ramm, Goma, Chair, peace commission for Kivu
- Cmdr. Peter, pilot for UNHCR, Goma
- Prof. Masumbuko, Chief Academic Officer, Centre of CAREP and member of Goma
- Dr. Kabuta-Biriage, Doctor of Theology, President of CAREP and member of Université libre des pays des Grands Lacs
- Mr. Batabiha Bushoki, President of the Peace Campaign and Secrétaire général of GEAD, Goma
- Prof. Kisangani Endanda, Recteur, Université d'Etat du Goma, Member, Peace Commission for Kivu, Goma
- Professor Arsene Kirhero, Innovation et réseaux pour le développement (IRED), Bukavu
- Mr. Bagenda Balagizi, Comité anti-Bwaki, groupe d'études et d'action politiques, Bukavu
- Ms. Josephine Kusinza, President, Association des femmes cadres pour l'épanouissement de la femme, Bukavu
- Mr. Ramazani Musongo, Fondation Rafad, Bukavu
- Mr. Mitima Mpanano, Programme d'appui aux initiatives de développement de Kivu, (PAIDEK), Bukavu
- Mr. Deogratias Liriza Olingi, Groupe Jeremie, Bukavu
- Mr. Pierre Cebambo, Catholic Relief Services (CARITAS), Bukavu

- Father Franco Bordegnon, Xaverienne Fathers, Bukavu
- Mr. Kalemba Tsongo, CRONGD, North Kivu, Executive Secretary, Goma
- Mr. Senzeyi Ryamukuru Leonard, former President of SIDER, and UMOJA, Goma
- Mr. Tabara Ernest, Campaign for Peace, Goma
- Mr. Barakengera Girimana, Campaign for Peace, Goma
- Dr. Clement Citeya Citeya, Political Science, Université de Kisangani, Kisangani
- Mr. François Lemba, Secretary for Information, Les amis de Nelson Mandela, Kisangani
- Mr. François Banza, Secretary for Analysis and Investigation, Les amis de Nelson Mandela, Kisangani
- Mr. Dismas Kitenga Senga, President, Group Lotus ONG des droits de l'homme et de développement, Kisangani
- Dr. Jean Otemicongo Mandefu, Chef de travaux, vice-doyen de la recherche à la faculté des Sciences sociales, administratives et politiques de l'université de Kisangani; also, Directeur, Centre d'éducation populaire aux droits de l'homme à la démocracie et au développement (CEPOD), Kisangani
- Dr. Nsaraza Nabintu Mme Professeur Obotela, Chef de travaux (Asst Professor), faculté de Médecine, Université de Kisangani; also, coordinator, Action féminine pour le développement communautaire, (AFDECO), Kisangani
- Father Guy Verhaegen, Paroisse Christ-Roi, Kisangani
- Mr. John Nsana, legal advisor to Secretary-General, ADFL, Kinshasa
- Mr. Rushoke, Kinshasa
- Col. James Kabareebe, Commander of the Army, Kinshasa.

www.ingramcontent.com/pod-product-compliance
Lightning Source LLC
Chambersburg PA
CBHW060347250426
43669CB00056B/2547